This journal book is full of inspiration to help
you through your healing process.  Life is full of
lessons enabling you to grow to a higher level of
consciousness.  This year will continue to give you
highs and lows but you will find your balance and
feel free again.

Month by Month; Step by Step

# Not all those who wander are lost

## Healing Journal Book

# People with clear, written goals accomplish far more than people without can ever imagine

### ~ My Goals ~

_____

_____

_____

_____

_____

_____

_____

_____

_____

_____

_____

_____

_____

_____

_____

_____

_____

_____

_____

_____

_____

_____

_____

_____

_____

_____

_____

_____

_____

_____

_____

_____

_____

_____

**Write 3 AMAZING things that happened to you today:**

1. _____

2. _____

3. _____

_____

_____

_____

_____

_____

_____

_____

_____

_____

_____

_____

_____

_____

_____

_____

_____

_____

# Password.
## Create a password to inspire you!

This will help you be mindful of your goal or maybe you want a new image of yourself?

Then it could be something like 'LOV3mys3lf' or maybe you want to save for your dream

holiday, then it could be 'SAVE4CRU1SE'.

Don't forget about your password hint: 'Be an Inspiration'

# Dream Journal

Go to your local book shop and buy a journal book to record your dreams. Dreams are another source of soul speak. Your soul speaks to you when your asleep this is when your highly receptive. Your soul can't tell the difference been your meditative state or if your sleeping. I'll teach you how to mediate soon. Now keep your dream journal and a pen beside your bed. It maybe helpful to have a lamp beside you incase you want to write down any dreams during the night.

Every morning before you get out of bed write down your dreams. Don't analysis them until after you have written them all down. Just write what ever your remember. There is no right or wrong, and don't worry about grammer.

Where were you in the dream?
Who were you with?
How did you feel?
Did you see any patterns or symbols?

As the days progress you will remember more, and if you don't it's ok because you will. Tonight before you go to sleep tell yourself you want to remember your dreams.

..you are not alone on this journey..

## *Buy Flowers*

Press your favourite flower; place it in this book, then use something heavy to weigh it down.

_____

_____

_____

_____

_____

_____

_____

_____

_____

_____

_____

_____

_____

Don't wait for someone else to give you what you need.
Buy your own flowers!  Why not, they make you happy, they smell lovely and they bring you joy.  Besides when was the last time someone brought you flowers?  Stop waiting.. this is your life.  Be happy, now, today!
You deserve it

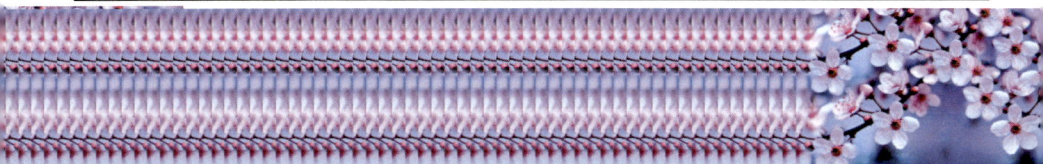

# ~ Find A Jar ~

Write on a piece of paper one thing you enjoy doing.... fill the jar with as many ideas as you can!  It doesn't have to be the big stuff it could just be things like:

~ having a bubble bath

~ walking along the beach or your local park - have a swing

~ search YouTube for inspiration:
                    learn to make soup? learn mixed media art?
~ skiing? sports? adventure?

~ host a dinner party

~ get out that sewing machine

~ check out your local hiking club

~ take time to watch your favourite programmes, and don't feel guilty about doing so!

~ bake something

~ colour in

~ going to the library

~ ringing a friend

~ painting with water colours, search YouTube for easy lessons

~ spend some time with your pet~ gardening / flower arranging

~ when was the last time you fixed something?

~ go to a movie during the day

Now at least once a week take out 1 idea out and do it.

Don't forget to keep adding to your jar & put your notes

back in for another day!!  Have fun with it.  This is

your life, your the leading role, make your story.

*.. everything is going to work out ..*

# Does your mind feel like a mess?

Do you keep repeating conversations over and over in your mind? or perhaps you focus on past events? Are you constantly worried & afraid about your future?

Find a comfortable place to sit down, grab your phone/ipad or laptop, any device you can watch a YouTube video on..you will need it soon.

Now, close your eyes and take a deep breath in, imagine beautiful light filling your body... hold your breath for 3 seconds.

Now breath out, letting go of anything negative, release it. Wanting these thoughts and horrible feelings to leave your body.

Pick up your phone/ipad or laptop, put it on do not disturb, and open YouTube. Search for 'Mediation for New Beginnings - How to Mediate for Beginners - BEXLIFE'. This is a good mediation video to start with. There are thousands on the internet, explore them. Listen to your gut feelings and play the videos that interest you.
Just remember Mediation is about calming your mind to help you fully relax. When you are taking deep breaths and your mind starts to wonder, that's ok just refocus on your breath, your stomach rising and falling.

If you don't have access to the internet, that's ok. Keep reading..
Count your breaths if it helps.
You need to stop running over the past in your mind...leave it there. It's done, you can't go back. Empty your mind. Concentrate only on your breath. Now Deep Breath in. Let go of the future, it will work out exactly how it's suppose to. Live in today, don't worry about tomorrow or the past.

Once you finish your meditation. It's time to plan your week ahead. Choose two things you love to do, that really light you up. Do them this week! What's to stop you? Nothing, your free to make your own choices. You can spend your time how ever you like! Make time. Your important too.

The way to happiness is letting go of anything you can't control, live in today, NOW, and trust that it will all work out.

_____

_____

_____

_____

_____

_____

_____

_____

_____

_____

_____

_____

_____

_____

_____

_____

_____

_____

_____

_____

Our thoughts are reflections of our reality. Thoughts are actually a passing event. Believing that they are the reflections of reality and holding onto them is at the origin of the suffering we can experience. Let go of negative thoughts, and re frame them in a positive way, a positive thought..

_____

_____

_____

_____

_____

_____

_____

_____

_____

_____

_____

_____

_____

_____

_____

*Stick post-it notes in places you will notice them. When you look at it, bring back your awareness to the present moment by breathing in and out for 10 breaths. Are you happy in this moment? If not, you have the power to Change it*

*Imagination and creativity gives us the tools to grow, to help us accept change.*

*Nothing stays still, we are constantly changing.*

*Everything around you is changing. Everyone is changing..*

*Do you remember being in a relationship where you felt uncomfortable? but stayed*

*You didn't want to lose what you had? That's you changing. Nothing stays the same.*

*Listen to your intuition, your gut feelings,*

*it's your soul speaking to you. It's telling you what you need to do.... walk away?*

*speak up? let go? You've changed!*

*Love is inside you, it's your thoughts, your feelings. Don't look for anyone else to give this to you.*
*Only you can make yourself happy.*

# Find Love in Food

Pancakes that will light up your Sunday morning.


- 1 teaspoon sea salt
- 1 1/2 cups self rising flower
- 1 1/4 cups whole milk, buttermilk or almond milk
- 1/2 cup plus 1 teaspoon olive oil or melted unsalted butter
- 2 large eggs
- 1 tablespoon granulated sugar
- 1 tablespoon vanilla extract
- Fresh fruit, and maple syrup, for serving
- Butter for fry pan


~ Turn on the oven to keep the pancakes warm ~


1. Whisk together the milk, 1/2 cup of the oil/ butter, and the eggs, sugar, and vanilla in a large bowl until the eggs are foamy and the sugar has dissolved.

2. Add the flour mixture to the milk mixture and stir until just mixed and moistened (the batter will be lumpy).

3.Heat a frying pan over medium heat. Once the pan is hot add 1 tablespoon of butter.

4. Pour pancake batter into the pan: 1/2 cup for large pancakes or 1/4 cup for smaller ones. Cook until bubbles completely cover the top, about 3 minutes. Flip and cook the other side until the bottoms are golden brown. Transfer the pancakes to the baking sheet in the oven to keep warm. Repeat with the remaining batter. Serve immediately with fresh fruit, butter, and maple syrup.

_____

_____

_____

_____

_____

_____

_____

_____

_____

_____

_____

_____

_____

_____

_____

_____

_____

_____

*Notice your environment.. take a picture of that positive moment. Whether it's the sun coming through the window, or a refreshing summer rain shower, it doesn't matter, as long as you take the time to acknowledge it and let the warming emotion unfold. It will allow you to experience the positive emotions again when you look at the photos again.*

# Your Goddess Smoothie

Your a Goddess who is in the process of learning to know, a woman who focuses on personal growth and self awareness accepts and loves herself - on all levels..
Mind Body & Spirit.

A  woman who is focusing on personal growth and self awareness, is experiencing a life increasingly filled with peace, love, joy, passion and fun.

 A woman that understands she has an unlimited capacity to make her life anything she wants.  A woman who is inspired to give to those around her, because of your sense of gratitude and abundance. This is your morning smoothie:

Ingredients:
* A handful of spinach leaves
* 1/2 an avocado
* 1/2 cup of blueberries
* 1 kiwifruit
* 1 tablespoon of ground flaxseed
* 1 banana
* almond milk

Put everything in your blender.
Use enough almond milk to
make it smooth (about cup).

write about what your scared of....

_____

_____

_____

_____

_____

_____

_____

_____

_____

_____

_____

_____

_____

_____

_____

_____

*Give yourself the life you want & deserve.*

### The power of receiving..

.if we are only givers, we wind up resentful and frustrated, often feeling taken advantage of.
..if we are only receivers, we become stagnate and selfish.

There needs to be balance "In order for there to be giving, there must be receiving, and in order for there to be receiving, there must be giving. "

...spices increase your metabolism...

1 buttercup pumpkin  just 200g provides a whole days vitamin C & vitamin A.  More dietary fiber than potatoes, carrots or even kiwifruit. Great energy source, holding 12% protein & 85% complex carbohydrates.  Excellent choice for weight watchers!

3 cloves garlic combats the common cold, can lower blood pressure, improves cholesterol levels & contains antioxidants. Garlic was one of the earliest 'performance enhancing' substances.

200ml water whether you want shinier hair, younger skin, a healthier body (or all 3), pure water is the world's best beauty elixier! Drink up

300ml almond milk is not dairy. It is a tasty diary-free, soy-free lactose-free alternative.  It's free of cholesterol and saturated (bad) fats.  Vitamin A is vital for healthy eye sight, vitamin E which plays a major role in improving your skin health, on account of it's antioxidant properties. Rich in vitamin B-12 which contributes to better muscle health. Contains several minerals and high in protein, thanks to almonds.

1 teaspoon cumin spice aids in the digestion, improves your immunity and treats insomnia, asthma, colds, skin disorders, boils and cancer.

1 teaspoon cinnamon lowers blood sugar levels, reduces heart disease risk factors.  It's the number 1 in antioxidant spices making it one of the healthiest spices on the planet!  Your body is better able to use your carbohydrate storage so that they do not turn into excess fat.

1 teaspoon allspice ease's digestive symptoms such as diarrhea, nausea & vomiting.  Traditionally this spice has been used to treat bacterial and fungal infections as well as coughs, chills, bronchitis and Depression. Yay!

Simmer in a pot (for about 1/2 hour) or until the pumpkin is soft.  Leave to cool a little, then zap in your blender. Bon Appetite x

I felt I was in a prison by my lack to dream big, to dream even a little more beyond what I already have! I haven't felt like I deserve any more than what life has gifted me so far. Where did i go? I used to have such big dreams when I was young.

When did I allow myself to become so suppressed by society? Always trying to fit in so I can be liked by everyone I meet! What an exhausting life to lead. Being truly you, it is the easiest thing you can do. You can't please everyone! And who cares, there are so many other people you haven't meet yet.

Have a go at this exercise. It's a just a small step, it will start to open your imagination. Try it. It's taken me over a year to reach the point where I feel I actually have something to write. Ever since this day I can't stop coming up with ideas!! Life is so exciting. You get to write your chapters, every day is a fresh start.

Pretend there are no limits, you have all the money in the world, nothing can stop you. You are a fictional character if you like.
What do you desire..

I am ...........................................................................................
...........................................................................................

I dream of ...................................................................................
...........................................................................................
...........................................................................................

I am talented for..........................................................................
...........................................................................................

What did the newspaper write about you.....................................
...........................................................................................
...........................................................................................

What's stopping you? ...................................................................

# Backwards Events

1. List 5 of your favourite things you do right now.

2. Pick one, your favourite one out of them all.

3. What was the last three events that guided you to doing this favourite thing?

4. Think back, what major bad event got you on to the path of doing your favourite thing?

Life's hardest times lead you to some of your most amazing things.

Start being grateful for having been through that hard time, because if that event didn't happen you wouldn't be doing what you love to do right now.

.. Rumi ..

God turns you from one feeling to another & teaches
by means of opposites so that you will have two
wings to fly, not one.

What is our life lesson/s?  What are you here for?  Big questions!

I've spent 3 years searching for these answers. I think we are here to learn lessons and to just enjoy life. I mean really be joyful.  I started doing things that made me happy, took some time to working out what actually lights up my soul, but each day I got a little better. During this time I had to allow myself to go through a grieving process (letting go of the past and forgiving them). Sounds easy aye! I was so scared, felt unbearable some days. Being the true you, authentic you, is the best thing you can do, its the only way you will be truly happy.

I have done so many brave things during this time.  Now it's your turn.

Next time your out and about notice: Is the frustrated mother at the checkout teaching you patience? or perhaps she's teaching you compassion?  Life is also about lessons.

Imagine if every person you meet was enlightened & you knew they were here to teach you something:

*Patience?  Independence?  Acceptance?  Compassion?*

~ meditate today ~

# Make a mind jar

*Fill an empty jar with hot water,*

*2 tablespoons of glitter glue & a few*

*drops of food colouring.*

*Shake the jar, this is your mind stressed, angry, & emotional.   Watch it settle, this is you calming down.*
*Meditation will help your mind to calm down.*

**A prayer for a sign**

*Thank you, angels, for sending me a sign of your loving presence in my life. It is good to know you are with me each step of the way.*

Download the 'Moon' app

# Reigniting
## your Creative thinking..

When you start to break your smallest patterns others begin to reveal themselves. When you force yourself to step outside of habit, you will begin to see your life from a new perspective.

O make your coffee a different way

O sit beside someone else in a meeting

O drive another way to work

O change your side of the bed

O have a bath in the morning

O read poetry, follow a poetry facebook page

O put your favourite music on when your in the shower

O ask your cafe to recommend a new drink flavour

O

O

O

Why would you need to control outcomes when YOU are the one making the rules?

*Matt Kahn*

# Nature is Beautiful

When was the last time you really noticed the beauty of nature?

Grab a cup of your favourite tea & a warm blanket. Go outside... Find somewhere comfortable, (I put an old couch outside under my favourite tree), Take notice of the sounds around you, take a few deep breaths in. How do you feel? Rest for a while, you have done enough.

You are heard, you are never alone.
Your life matters.
Good things are coming your way, believe it.
How do you feel?

What season is your life in right now?
What things do you enjoy about this season?

What is one thing you can do tomorrow to make it better? Listen to your soul, your gut feelings, you know what you need to do.

*Smile, you don't have to hide anymore!*

Success is getting up in the mornings, going to bed at night, and in between you get to do what you want to do, what you enjoy doing. Work should be doing what you love.

Ring the florist - order flowers to be delivered to yourself on valentines day with a note "Happy Valentines"

*~ today just be ~*

.. let the tears flow ..
time to heal ..

...unless we fully enter into the direct experience of our soul wounds,
we can not go beyond them...

~Turn off push notifications to your mobile phone today~

... you are so loved ...

*Bliss*
lies in
balance

...the key to keeping your balance is knowing when you lose it...

# make a list of things that make you smile

could be something your pet did ..

_Go Back ..... think back to what make your eyes sparkle as a child.  Was it going to the zoo to see the animals, or having a box full of new crayons and a blank piece of paper? Whatever it was, your passion won't have left you, so go back and see what you can reclaim right now._

_____

_____

_____

_____

_____

_____

_____

_____

_____

_____

_____

_____

_____

_____

_____

_____

**A pray for healing & love**

*Thank you, divine healing angels, for supporting me as I release
the thoughts that no longer serve me, so I can align with my soul's
truth, which is whole, complete and healed.
I align myself with love x*

*"writing can't change the story, but it can change how you think about it"* J Connor, 2008.

*Becoming more of an observer in your life and using writing to capture your observations can provide you not only with insights but also with new ways of viewing difficult and challenging situations.*

_____

_____

_____

_____

_____

_____

_____

_____

_____

_____

_____

_____

_____

_____

_____

_____

_____

Only do what your heart tells you.

- Princess Diana

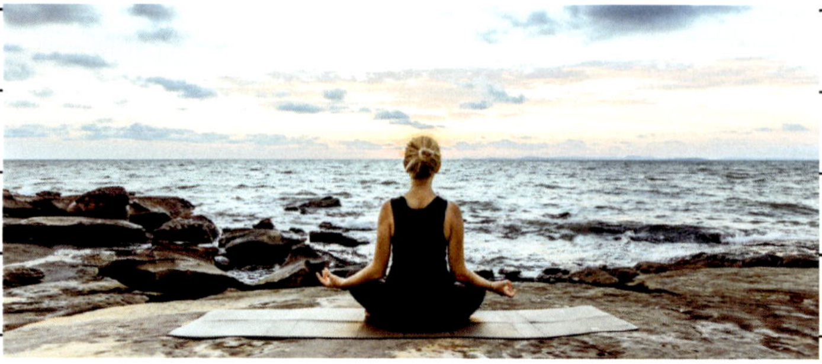

Exploring your Chakras:

Crown Chakra ~ violet or white, located at the very top of your head, represents your spirituality and connection to your life purpose.

Third Eye Chakra ~ indigo colour, located on your forehead between the eyes, represents your creativity, intuition, and intelligence.

Throat Chakra ~ blue or turquoise, is in your throat area, represents your expression an communication of your inner will.

Heart Chakra ~ green, located in the center of your chest, just above your heart, represents your heart center, intuition, and self love.

Solar Plexus Chakra ~ yellow, located in your upper abdomen, stomach area, represents your identity, personality, and self esteem.

Sacral Chakra ~ orange, located in your lower abdomen, about 2 inches below the navel and 2 inches in, represents your sexuality, personal power, and relationships.

Root Chakra ~ red, located at the base of your spine in the tailbone area, represents your family connection, and foundations of your emotional and mental centers.

_____

_____

_____

_____

_____

_____

_____

_____

_____

_____

_____

_____

_____

_____

*Exercise: Looking at your own aura*

*when your lying in bed tomorrow morning, do this exercise when you have just woken up so your nice and relaxed.  1. Raise your hand above your face and gaze at it. 2. Gaze at your middle finger and allow yourself to go into a trance/dream like state, you'll begin to see your aura developing all around your hand. 3. If you don't see colour, close your eyes and see what colours swirl around in your mind.  The more your practice the easier it is to see! Ask your guides to show you the colour.*

## Aura Colours:

- **Purple:** this color means you're connected with spiritual thoughts.
- **Blue:** it symbolises a balanced existence, sustaining life, eased nerve system, transmitting forces and energy.
- **Turquoise:** indicates dynamic quality of being, highly energised personality, capable of projection, and influencing other people.
- **Green:** like the earth, this color is a restorative aura. It signifies restful, modifying energy, and natural healing abilities.
- **Yellow:** people with yellow auras are full of joy, freedom, generous, non-attachment, and freeing or releasing vital forces.
- **Orange:** this means a person who is uplifting, absorbing, or inspiring. Orange aura can be a sign of power and the ability and/or desire to control people.
- **Red:** a red aura can be somewhat of a red flag, as this means a focus on materialistic thoughts or about the physical body.
- **Pink:** this aura color means spiritual love, and is no easy feat. To obtain a clean pink aura, you need to mix the purple, the highest frequency we perceive, with the lowest, which is red.

_____

_____

_____

_____

_____

_____

_____

_____

_____

_____

_____

_____

*..you deserve love..*

We are not responsible for what we see,

but we are responsible for how we perceive

*Watch an old black & white movie. Get comfy on the couch with snacks & a nourishing drink*

...keep trying keep growing...

Elephants with their trunks down are thought to be accumulating positive energy and pushing through obstacles, and are particularly potent totems for those seeking fertility, wisdom, or strength.

..the universe works fast when your having fun..

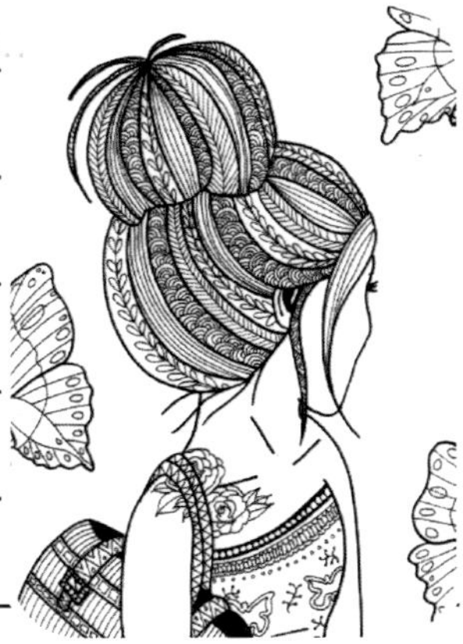

# Learn Tarot Cards

**Tarot is the storybook of our life, the mirror to our soul, and the key to our inner wisdom.**

Simply ask a question, pull a card, to give you instant access to your inner wisdom and the answer you need.

_...everything will come to you just when you need it..._

Using a **Pendulum** is a simple way to access Divine guidance, and they are very accurate, if used correctly.

You will first need to find out how it wants to communicate its answers to you. You will need a "yes", a "no", and a "maybe" answer, and if you want, "I don't want to answer that".

In order to be sure that your answers are accurate, sit down at a desk or table, so there is support under your elbow.
To begin using a pendulum, hold it in your dominant hand. I like to loop my chain over my index finger with the end of the chain between my thumb and index finger, and the pendulum swinging freely.

**Start by saying aloud, "I wish to connect to my higher self." I feel that by speaking these words, this gives notice to my guides that we are beginning, and lets me know that I have connected.**

First you would ask "Please show me yes," and wait for its response. If the pendulum does not move, it means that you have got no response.
In that case simply continue on. Next you ask, "Show me no." Some pendulums like to answer that one first. Usually the pendulum will move a certain way. If you get no response to either question you could make a decision and speak it aloud, for example "Yes is ..."
In my case the pendulum showed me:

• No as.... moving in a big circle.
• Yes as.... moving backwards and forwards.
• Maybe as.... moving in a tiny circle, similar to yes but barely moving.
• I don't want to answer... this varies. Sometimes it will move all over the place... or stay perfectly still... not moving at all.
**When** closing off your session always show Gratitude and say "Thank You".

*If your pendulum is made from any type of crystal, please remember that it is important to cleanse your crystal regularly.*

**Here are some 9 great fennel seed benefits:**

- Helps Regulate Blood Pressure: ...
- Reduce Water Retention : ...
- **Fennel** Tea for Constipation, Indigestion, IBS & Bloating: ...
- **Fennel Seeds** Reduce Asthma Symptoms : ...
- Helps Purify Blood: ...
- Improves Eyesight: ...
- According to Ayurveda: ...
- Great for Acne:

This is no dress rehearsal,
so stop worrying and enjoy the show

What happened to that little inside you? Where did she go? I meet someone once who told me there is a 'print' for you every year as you grow older. So it's easy to revisit yourself at any age. Close your eyes and remember the 5 year old you, if this is hard go to your photo album find a photo of you when you were a little girl and happy. Now close your eyes and remember her......imagine taking her to the safest place you can imagine, could be a forest or an island. Sit with her a while, give her a hug, tell her you love her, maybe play with her a while. Anytime you are down, close your eyes and imagine her there; happy, playing, not a care in the world. You are safe & so dearly loved xx

Deep breath, Smile

..don't forget to look up..

..put a vase of rosemary on your desk..

# TITANIC'S PASSENGERS SAVED; LINER SINKING

## ILL-FATED VESSEL BEGINS TO FOUNDER WHILE LIMPING
## TOWARD HALIFAX AFTER ALL ABOARD ARE RESCUED

### WAR WITH MEXICO NEAR

**State Department Note Brings About Crisis; Answer Is Anxiously Awaited**

**Orozco to Be Judged by Deeds Rather Than by Promises; Americans to Arm**

WASHINGTON, April 15.—The State Department's formal note to the contending factions in Mexico, warning them against any mistreatment of Americans, is believed to have brought the relations between the United States and Mexico to the critical point. This is a fair deduction from past experience and tradition of the State Department, notably and recently in the case of Cuba.

It is recalled that such warning as this preceded the Spanish-American war, culminating in the famous message of President McKinley which referred "no intolerable conditions existing at our doorway."

It still is hoped and believed by administration officials, however, that Saturday's notes will have a sobering effect on the revo...

Giant Liner Titanic of the White Star Line, which collided with an iceberg last night in midocean while on her maiden voyage.

### Monster of Ocean Badly Damaged by Collision With Iceberg; Many Notables on List

### Wireless Calls for Help Crash Out in Night, Calling Greyhounds of Sea to Stand By

**BULLETIN**

HALIFAX, N. S., April 15. — The Canadian government marine agency here at 4:15 p. m. received a wireless dispatch that the Titanic is sinking. The message came via the cable ship Minia off Cape Race. It is said the vessels towing the Titanic were endeavoring to get her into shoal water near Cape Race to beach her.

**BULLETIN.**

NEW YORK, April 15.—Vice-President Franklin of the White Star Line said at 4 o'clock that he had definite information that all the passengers had been transferred from the Titanic. He had received nothing, however, indicating the extent of the damage to the liner.

WIRELESS dispatches up to noon today showed that the passengers of the White Star liner Titanic, which

Peacock symbolise **Vision** (in Greco-Roman mythology the Peacock tail has the 'eyes' of the stars), **Royalty** (guardian to royalty, it is seen in engravings upon thrones), **Spirituality, Awakening, Guidance, Immortality** (The feathers are talismans to protect the wearer from accidents, poisoning, diseases, and other disasters.)**Protection, & Watchfulness.** The Peacock feather represents immortality, and can absorb negative energies, protecting those who wear them.

**The Peacock is a reminder to all of us to show our true colors.**

_____

_____

_____

_____

_____

_____

_____

*Single doesn't always mean lonely, and
relationships don't always mean happiness*

..you have so much to offer..

_____

_____

_____

_____

_____

_____

_____

_____

_____

_____

_____

_____

_____

_____

Closing down your Chakra's

This is very important, as it allows you to retain your energy and not leave yourself **vulnerable** to wandering energies, particularly before you go to sleep!

* Close your eyes and see your guardian angel behind you, your golden light of protection all around you.

* Imagine your closing your 7 chakra's, think about them like a flower if you like, and your closing the flower petals to a bud again.

* Take a few minutes to be grateful, and thank your angels for the messages they have sent you.

*...when was the last time you brought yourself a gift...*

Meditation for Self **LOVE**

Close your eyes and take some deep breaths.
Keep breathing for a few minutes until you feel yourself
relaxing completely.

Relax your forehead, relax your legs & relax your shoulders.....

Imagine yourself standing opposite you.  When your ready, tell
her you love her, send her warm loving light.  Tell her she no
longer has to feel pain or guilt.  She has done nothing wrong.
Imagine sending her light so she starts to feel powerful.

*Say:*

*"You are powerful"*
*"You are beautiful"*
*"You are love"*

*"I am powerful"*
*"I am beautiful"*
*"I am love"*

Take a deep breath, and let the feelings wash over you.  Be still
for a few more minutes, feel the power within you.  When your
ready open your eyes xox

_____

_____

_____

_____

_____

_____

_____

_____

# Grounding Ritual after Yoga or Mediation:
Place hands in to a prayer pose.

* Bring your hands to your heart, say "to the highest love"

* Bring your hands to your lips, say " to the highest truth"

* Now touch your prayer hands to your forehead, say "to the highest

consciousness - I give mine"

_____

_____

_____

_____

_____

_____

_____

_____

_____

_____

_____

_____

_____

_____

_____

_____

_____

_____

## Today's Affirmations..

I make ideas happen

I create what no one has created before

I learn what I need to learn, when I need to learn it

I make this happen

I am a super creator

_____

_____

_____

_____

_____

_____

_____

_____

_____

_____

_____

_____

_____

_____

_____

Your business idea won't be completely new, it doesn't have to be. Most ideas have already been done. Instead recognise your passion, recognise the gap in the market, and solve it!

Working in an area you have passion for and solving that problem is a powerful mix.

What am I afraid of ..

How do I attack myself ..

How do I attack others ..

How do I bring my past fears into the present ..

*Wake up thinking of 5 things to be grateful for.  Your bed, your*
*food, your loved ones, your car ..*

*..not all storms come to disrupt your life,*
*some come to clear the path..*

*.. you make a difference in the world..*

_____

_____

_____

_____

_____

_____

_____

_____

_____

_____

_____

_____

_____

_____

_____

_____

_____

_____

To avoid criticism, do nothing, say nothing, be nothing.

Elbert Hubbard

_____

_____

_____

_____

_____

_____

_____

_____

_____

_____

_____

_____

_____

_____

_____

_____

_____

_____

Our ego wants us to stay right where we are, where survival is guaranteed.  Listen to your higher self instead.

What is your business idea?
* what is your idea called?
* how does it meet peoples needs?
* what are the benefits for people?
* research today

*What happened today?*

_____

_____

_____

_____

_____

_____

_____

_____

_____

_____

_____

_____

_____

_____

_____

_____

I used to think as I looked out on the Hollywood night - there must be thousands of girls sitting alone like me, dreaming of becoming a movie star. But I'm not going to worry about them. I'm dreaming the hardest.

Marilyn Munroe

.. I am loving awareness ..

*Make a play list of your favourite songs*

# Be Authentic

Being yourself is not about standing out or being different from others. Being authentic is following your path, not comparing to others. When you try to be 'different,' you disconnect from what *you* want.

Try these steps:

#1 Assume Intimacy from the beginning: Talk to strangers like you would talk to a real friend. Don't treat a first date like a job interview, imagine it is a 3rd date instead. And see your job interviewer as an existing colleague instead of an intimidating new boss.

#2 Don't try to appeal to everyone: Your vibe attracts your tribe. You are original, don't water yourself down. Don't be a people pleaser, find your people and speak directly to them.

#3 Difficult people are difficult because of their fears. Take a chance. Start honoring the authentic, true you and sharing that more openly with the world. Share something a little deep. Don't try so hard to cover your imperfections. Use vulnerability as a bonding mechanism. Don't apologise for what you feel or think, assert your boundaries and say "no" where you need to.

Start sharing more of the real you with the world, and you'll find that you'll become strong enough to deal with the consequences, and lead a happier life.

## Time to start dancing in the shower!

*2 songs minimum*

_____

_____

_____

_____

_____

_____

_____

_____

_____

_____

_____

_____

_____

_____

_____

_____

_____

_____

## Buy Eyeshadow Primer

_____

_____

_____

_____

_____

_____

_____

_____

_____

_____

_____

_____

_____

_____

_____

_____

_____

Primer is a must-have product that should be applied before any makeup products, especially eyeshadow. Think about it: What's worse than creating a perfect masterpiece on your eyes, only to have it crease, fade or smudge just an hour or so later? Nothing.

Like face primer, eye primer ensures your eyeshadow or liquid eyeliner stays put all day long and prevents your shadow from creasing on your eyelids.

# Grateful Day.

On waking tomorrow, before you open your
eyes, thank your bed for a good nights sleep.

*It's the little things in life* ♡

_____

_____

_____

_____

_____

_____

_____

_____

_____

_____

_____

_____

_____

_____

_____

_____

_____

**Mirror Work Day**

**Look in the mirror.**

**Say**

**"life loves me"**

"In my room I have a mirror, and I call it my Magic Mirror. Inside this mirror is my very best friend."

Louise Hay

Do you remember kissing yourself in the mirror as a little girl? Mirror work helps you to love yourself again. When you love yourself, you see that life loves you too.

# Let's make a smoothie for breakfast

### 1/2 banana
**(keep them frozen so they last longer)**
### 1/2 cup of your favourite berries
**(from the freezer)**
### 1 1/4 cup Milk
**(almond milk, cashew milk, or coconut milk)**
### 1/2c pro biotic yoghurt
**(greek yoghurt)**

**In a blender, combine all ingredients and blend until smooth.
Use paper straws from the supermarket.**

as you
start to
walk out
on the way
the way
appears

-Rumi

Only from the heart
can you touch the sky
~ Rumi

... I am blessed ...

.. I step back and let the universe lead the way..

.. I am loved ..

.. I focus my attention on the love that is around me ..

.. I am light ..

The question isn't who is going to let me; it's who is going to stop me.
— Ayn Rand

~Take regular breaks after blocks of focused attention~

*By giving yourself permission to stop, and by accepting that rest is actually a highly productive activity, you can come back to your tasks with new energy and insight*

_____

_____

_____

_____

_____

_____

_____

_____

_____

_____

_____

_____

_____

_____

_____

_____

_____

_____

save to buy eyelash growth serum

**Get long eyelashes naturally:** Put olive oil or coconut oil on your eyelashes. These oils are known to strengthen and stimulate eyelash growth. Apply olive or coconut oil on your eyelids and on the skin under your eyes every night (before you go to bed) for a noticeable effect.

.. surrender to the now ..

"Every fleet of ships that sails has a mothership; one ship that knows where all of them are going and sets the direction for all of those ships to sail. This doesn't mean that the mothership determines what happens on each of the other ships in the fleet.

Life on one of the ships might be mostly pleasant. On yet another ship, it might be mostly unpleasant. Now imagine the mothership is the biggest ship you can imagine, it's a city afloat, *magnificent*.

**Now imagine** that the rest of the ships aren't really ships, but they're little boats. The mothership is your soul and you are one of the little boats. The mothership knows why you are in the water. You may not know all of the time. The mothership knows why you encounter storms. *Your job, while you have the awesome privilege of being a little boat, is to learn how to learn how to sail in the same direction as your mothership.* Because you can choose and create anything you want, you can sail in the opposite direction, if you want.

That is a sure way to find rough water. But as you sail in the direction that your mothership wants to sail; your life fills with meaning, and purpose, and love. You are excited about being alive. You are excited about the people that you're with and what you are doing.

Meaning is your inner compass that always aligns itself with the direction that your mothership wants to go. As you follow your inner sense of meaning, you are sailing in the same direction your mothership wants to sail."

–Gary Zukav

your wings already exist.
All you have to do is
fly.

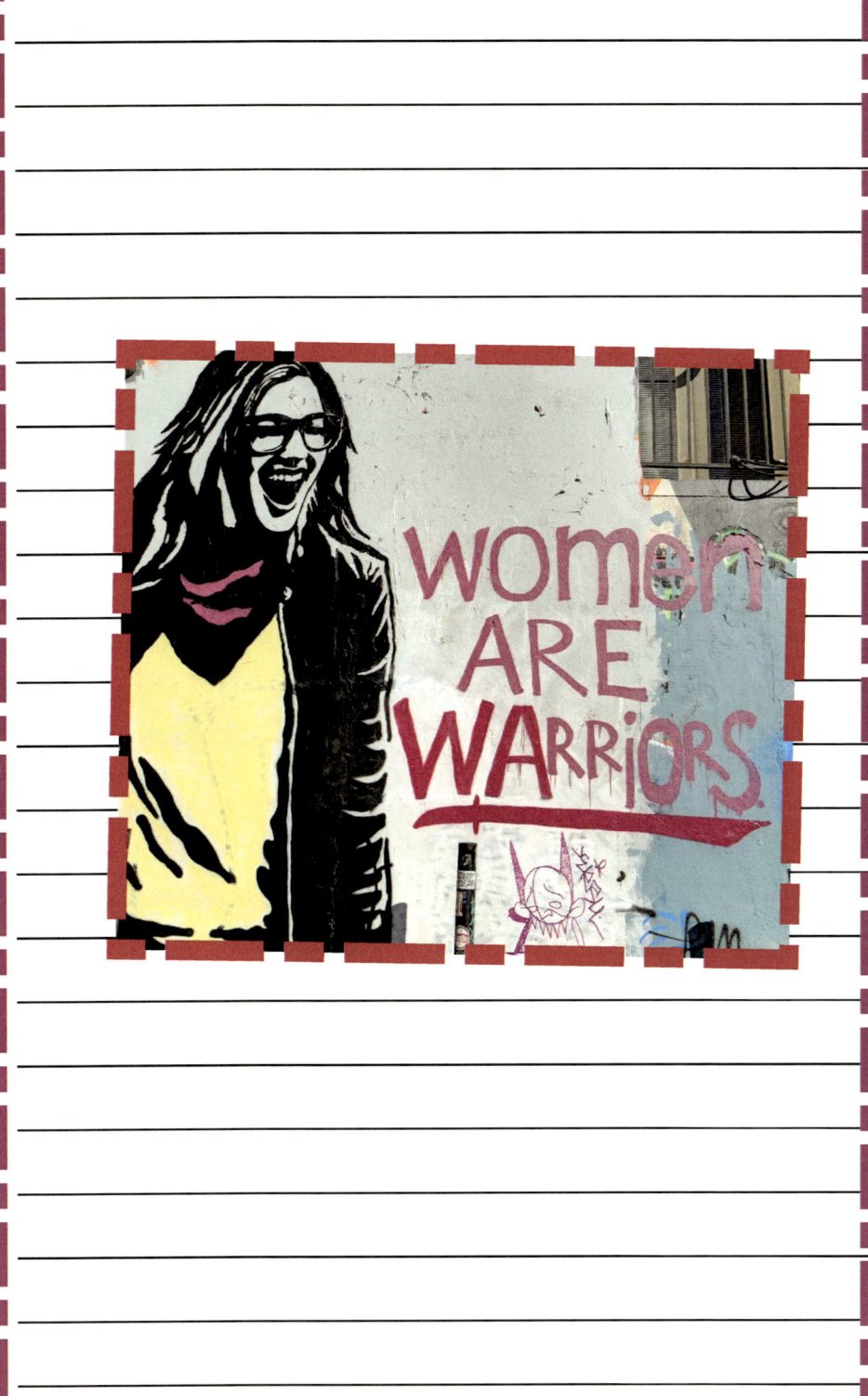

This website is for people who enjoy sending and receiving *postcards* from people all around the *world*. You send 5 postcards to start, once they are received by people, the website randomly selects 5 people to send you postcards and so on. *Real* postcards too!

_____

_____

_____

_____

_____

_____

_____

_____

_____

_____

_____

_____

_____

_____

_____

_____

_____

_____

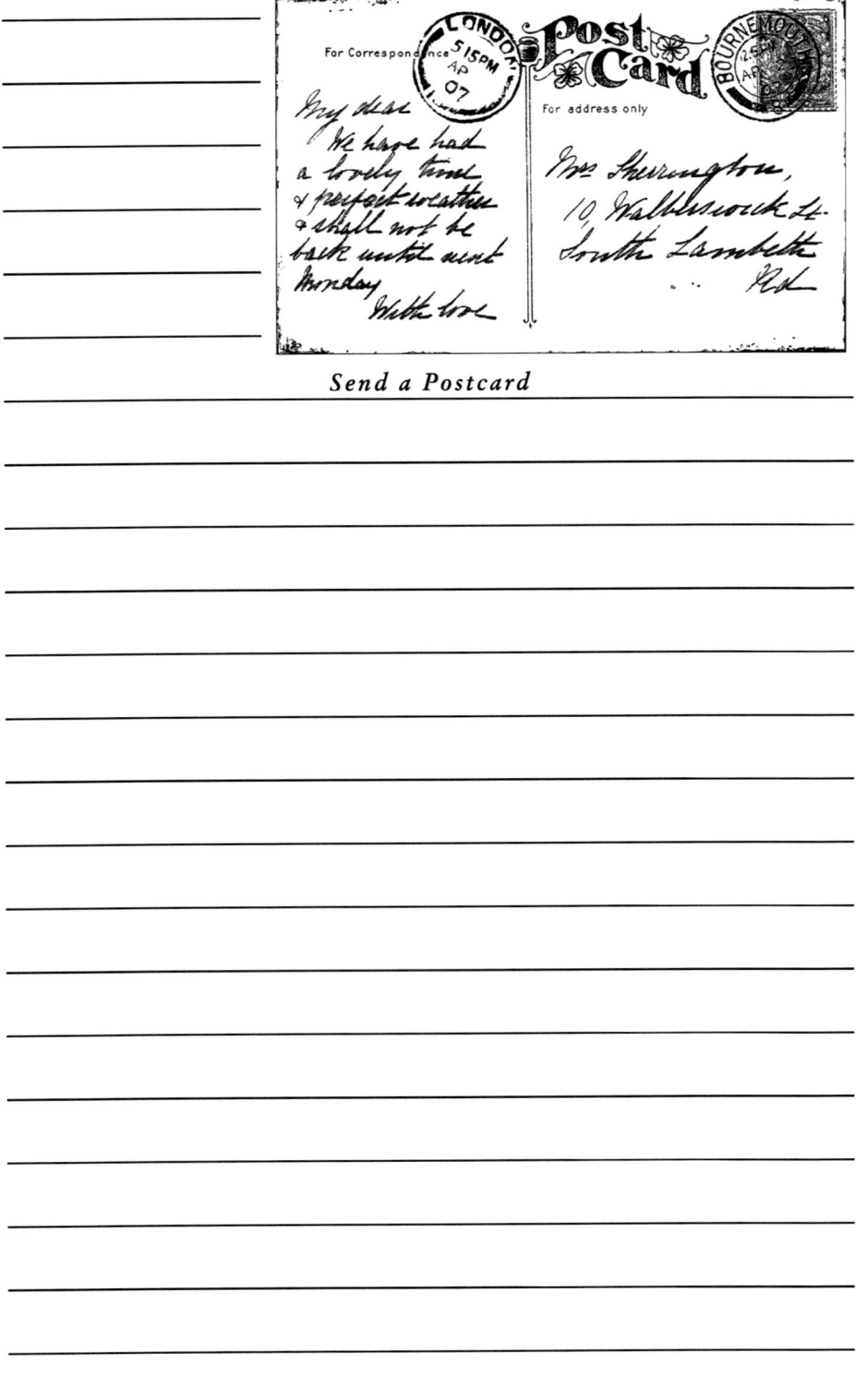

*Send a Postcard*

It's ok to feel angry. It's an emotion we all should feel. It's what you choose to do with it that matters.  Punch a boxing bag, go for a run, write a letter then burn it, scream as loud as you can! Release, it feels so good.

_____

_____

_____

_____

_____

_____

_____

_____

_____

_____

_____

_____

_____

_____

_____

_____

_____

_____

_____

_____

_____

_____

...WILL I REGRET IT IF I DON'T DO IT...

Make a bookmark today

~maybe it's time to be shine again~

~you can~

Design a colourful
face from cardboard

"people want what they want. Sometimes you just have to
**WALK IN DEFIANCE** of it and **JUST BE YOURSELF**."
- Meryl Streep

*...the best thing about the future is that*

*it comes one day at a time ...*

*~and she did it anyway~*

*A good friend is . . .*

Fun to be around

Trustworthy

Supportive

Non-judgmental

~Embrace silence and create a space for nothing today~

*~be a rebel and walk away from negativity~*

*"life is wonderful, so eat the damn red velvet cupcake"*

*- Emma Stone*

## Shower Meditation.

Every time you take a shower visualise washing away your stress and anxiety. Concentrate on the feeling of the water upon your skin. Envision the power of the shower washing away your negative thoughts. Woosh! Envision fear, regret and anger soaping off you and swirling down the drain...

_____

_____

_____

_____

_____

_____

_____

_____

_____

_____

_____

_____

_____

_____

_____

_____

_____

_____

_____

Are you feeling pain? Ask your higher self
"what unconscious thoughts are creating tension
in my body".  Take a few deep breaths.

Do some research, what ever comes to your mind.
 Google that.  What is your higher self trying to show you?  Work
through the triggers that are creating this resistance. This is a
hard task but you need to face your fears.  What is controlling
you?  What are you scared of?  Do you want to continue on this
destructive path?  You can't, your body will get sicker.

Take some time over the next couple of days to trust your
instincts, your higher self is trying to help you release.  Let the
tears flow. It's going to be so worth it!

*~you already know..   trust yourself~*

*~ there is so much good to see ~*

_____

_____

_____

_____

_____

_____

_____

*"I alone cannot change the world,*
*but I can cast a stone across the waters to create many ripples."*

*- Mother Teresa*

_____

_____

_____

_____

_____

_____

_____

_____

_____

_____

_____

_____

_____

_____

*Junk Journal day... google Junk Journal or search youtube. It's a great way of making a gift to yourself.*

*What is your journal theme?*

*Animals, flowers, family, sports, astrology, wedding, cooking, or interior design?*

Dear Destiny,

I know you are held within my heart, I ask you to open and allow your wings to spread, let yourself be free to fly, believe in the beautiful magic within.  Dream BIG, and never ever give up.

*You are so loved xox*

Lightning Source UK Ltd.
Milton Keynes UK
UKRC020946290720
367276UK00013BC/165